This book is for ....

....

With love from ....

....

PaRragon.

IN THE BEGINNING

OUR FAMILY TREE

PLACE PHOTO HERE

Maternal Great Grandmother

PLACE PHOTO HERE

Maternal Great Grandfather

PLACE PHOTO HERE

Maternal Great Grandmother

PLACE PHOTO HERE

Maternal Great Grandfather

PLACE PHOTO HERE

Maternal Grandmother

PLACE PHOTO HERE

Maternal Grandfather

PLACE PHOTO HERE

Mother

PLACE PHOTO HERE

Me, age ....

PLACE PHOTO HERE

Paternal Great Grandmother

PLACE PHOTO HERE

Paternal Great Grandfather

PLACE PHOTO HERE

Paternal Great Grandmother

PLACE PHOTO HERE

Paternal Great Grandfather

PLACE PHOTO HERE

Paternal Grandmother

PLACE PHOTO HERE

Paternal Grandfather

PLACE PHOTO HERE

Father

PLACE PHOTO HERE

Me, age ....

MY GREAT-GRANDPARENTS

My mom's maternal grandparents were

Grandmother .... Heritage ....

Grandfather .... Heritage ....

Their story ....

....

....

My mom's paternal grandparents were

Grandmother .... Heritage ....

Grandfather .... Heritage ....

Their story ....

....

....

My dad's maternal grandparents were

Grandmother .... Heritage ....

Grandfather .... Heritage ....

Their story ....

....

....

My dad's paternal grandparents were

Grandmother .... Heritage ....

Grandfather .... Heritage ....

Their story ....

....

....

PLACE
PHOTO HERE

PLACE
PHOTO HERE

MY GRANDPARENTS

On Mom's side

Grandpa was named ....

He was born in .... on ....

His family members were ....

....

His job was ....

Grandma was called ....

She was born in .... on ....

Her family members were ....

....

Her job was ....

On Dad's side

Grandpa was named ....

He was born in .... on ....

His family members were ....

....

His job was ....

Grandma was called ....

She was born in .... on ....

Her family members were ....

....

Her job was ....

PLACE
PHOTO HERE

PLACE
PHOTO HERE

PLACE
PHOTO HERE

FIRST MEMORIES

I was born on .... at ....

I was named ....

My mom was named ....

My dad was named ....

My mom worked as a ....

My dad worked as a ....

My first address was ....

....

My earliest memory is ....

....

....

....

Major events that happened the year I was born were ....

....

....

....

A DAY I REMEMBER FONDLY...

PLACE
PHOTO HERE

This is ....

....

....

STORIES FROM MY FAMILY

On my birth

My temperament as a baby was

How my mother coped with motherhood:

How my father coped with fatherhood:

PLACE
PHOTO HERE

This is ....
....
....

STORIES FROM MY FAMILY

PLACE
PHOTO HERE
PLACE
PHOTO HERE

EARLY YEARS

WHEN I WAS A GIRL...

A can of soda cost $......................

A candy bar cost $......................

A loaf of bread cost $......................

A gallon of milk cost $......................

A movie ticket cost $......................

An average salary was $......................

An average car cost $......................

A family home cost $......................

The president was ....

The most popular TV show was ....

The most popular movie star was ....

The most popular singer was ....

PLACE
PHOTO HERE

PLACE
PHOTO HERE

ELEMENTARY SCHOOL DAYS

My first school was named ....

My favorite teacher was named ....

My friends were named ....

....

My favorite subject was ....

....

What I liked about school was ....

....

....

What I didn't like about school was ....

....

....

I was always getting into trouble for ....

....

....

....

The funniest thing that happened at school was ....

....

....

....

....

....

PLACE
PHOTO HERE

Me at school, age ....

SCHOOL DAYS

The best thing about school was

PLACE
PHOTO HERE

PLACE
PHOTO HERE

MY FRIENDS

My best friends were

We would spend our time

The funniest thing we did was

They probably would describe me as

PLACE
PHOTO HERE

PLACE
PHOTO HERE

PLACE
PHOTO HERE

PLACE
PHOTO HERE

PLACE
PHOTO HERE

PLACE
PHOTO HERE

MY FAVORITES AS A GIRL

Songs

Movies

TV shows

Radio stations

Sports

Actors

Actresses

Colors

Books

Foods

Outfits

PLACE
PHOTO HERE

PLACE
PHOTO HERE

PLACE
PHOTO HERE

PLACE
PHOTO HERE

PLACE
PHOTO HERE

PLACE
PHOTO HERE

A DAY I REMEMBER FONDLY...

GROWING UP

FAMILY VACATIONS

A typical family vacation would be

We would often go to

My favorite vacation was to

The thing I loved to do on vacation was

PLACE
PHOTO HERE

PLACE
PHOTO HERE

PLACE
PHOTO HERE

PLACE
PHOTO HERE

PLACE
PHOTO HERE

PLACE
PHOTO HERE

BIRTHDAY PARTIES

In our house, we always celebrated birthdays by

My mom or dad would always make

One particular party I will always remember was

My favorite gift was

My favorite party game was

BIRTHDAY PARTIES

The most fun party was

PLACE
PHOTO HERE

PLACE
PHOTO HERE

PLACE
PHOTO HERE

HIGH SCHOOL

My high school was named ....

My favorite subject was ....

....

....

....

My favorite teacher was ....

....

I was a .... kind of student.

When I was in high school I wanted to be ....

....

....

....

....

My best high school memory was

PLACE
PHOTO HERE

PLACE
PHOTO HERE

FRIENDS AND HOBBIES

My best friends were

We would spend our time together

The hobbies we shared were

Our favorite things to do together were

PLACE
PHOTO HERE

PLACE
PHOTO HERE

PLACE
PHOTO HERE

A picture of my house, taken in ....

WHERE I LIVED

My address was ....

....

....

I would describe my childhood home as ....

....

....

....

My favorite part of the house was ....

....

....

....

....

PLACE
PHOTO HERE

MY FAVORITES AS A TEENAGER

Songs ....

Movies ....

TV shows ....

Times of day ....

Sports ....

Actors ....

Actresses ....

Colors ....

Books ....

Foods ....

Outfits ....

PLACE
PHOTO HERE

PLACE
PHOTO HERE

PLACE
PHOTO HERE

PLACE
PHOTO HERE

INTO ADULTHOOD

PLACE
PHOTO HERE
PLACE
PHOTO HERE

GRADUATION

I graduated high school on ....

I celebrated by ....

....

....

....

....

....

....

....

....

....

....

....

....

....

....

....

PLACE
PHOTO HERE
PLACE
PHOTO HERE

AFTER GRADUATION

After high school, I went on to ....

STARTING MY CAREER

My first job was

My salary was

I spent my first paycheck on

I liked working because

Although I didn't like

Working for a living taught me

PLACE
PHOTO HERE

PLACE
PHOTO HERE

PLACE
PHOTO HERE

PLACE
PHOTO HERE

PLACE
PHOTO HERE

LOVE AND MARRIAGE

MEETING GRANDPA

I first met Grandpa

My first thoughts were

When my parents first met him, they

While we dated, we

Back then, the thing I loved about him most was

PLACE
PHOTO HERE
PLACE
PHOTO HERE

PLACE
PHOTO HERE

GRANDPA AND I WERE MARRIED...

Date

Time

Place

We had our reception at

We ate

Our first dance was

My dress was

PLACE
PHOTO HERE

PLACE
PHOTO HERE

ABOUT THE DAY

It was special because

PLACE
PHOTO HERE

PLACE
PHOTO HERE

PLACE
PHOTO HERE

PLACE
PHOTO HERE

OUR HONEYMOON

After we got married, we went on our honeymoon to ....
....
....

We traveled by ....

We were away for ....

My fondest memory is when ....
....
....
....
....
....
....
....

My favorite part of the honeymoon was when ....
....
....
....
....
....
....
....
....

PLACE
PHOTO HERE

PLACE
PHOTO HERE

OUR FIRST HOME

Our first home together was at

We lived there for

In the first year of marriage we spent our time

The times I cherish the most are

A FAMILY OF
MY OWN

PREGNANCY AND BIRTH

I found out I was first pregnant in ....

....

....

When I found out I felt ....

....

....

My pregnancy was ....

....

....

I loved being pregnant because ....

....

....

But the worst thing about being pregnant was ....

....

....

PLACE
PHOTO HERE

PLACE
PHOTO HERE

PLACE
PHOTO HERE

MY CHILDREN GROWING UP

The thing I loved the most about being a mother back then was

My children loved to play

As a family, we would

PLACE
PHOTO HERE

PLACE
PHOTO HERE

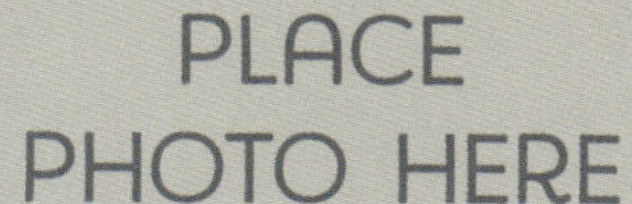

PLACE
PHOTO HERE

PLACE
PHOTO HERE

FAMILY VACATION

As a family, we would go on vacation to

The children liked to

Grandpa would always

A typical vacation would be

PLACE
PHOTO HERE

PLACE
PHOTO HERE

My favorite vacation with my family was when we went to ....
....
....
....
....
....
....
....
....

PLACE
PHOTO HERE

....

My funniest vacation moment was when ....
....
....
....
....
....
....
....
....

....

HOLIDAY SEASON

Holidays were always ....

....

We would celebrate by ....

....

....

Our visitors would be ....

....

....

We would eat ....

....

....

We would drink ....

....

....

Our favorite traditions were ....

....

....

....

....

PLACE
PHOTO HERE

PLACE
PHOTO HERE

My funniest memory was when ....

....

....

....

....

....

....

....

....

PLACE
PHOTO HERE

....

My favorite year was when ....
....
....
....
....
....
....
....
....

PLACE
PHOTO HERE

....

PLACE
PHOTO HERE

PLACE
PHOTO HERE

PLACE
PHOTO HERE

PLACE
PHOTO HERE

THE NEXT STAGE

MY CHILDREN LEAVING HOME

My last child left home in

I initially felt

I decided I would spend my time

PLACE
PHOTO HERE

PLACE
PHOTO HERE

PLACE
PHOTO HERE

TIME TO OURSELVES

Once our children left home, we spent our time

We went on vacation by ourselves again to

We enjoyed this time because

By this time, Grandpa worked as a

I worked as a

We spent time with our friends

MY HOBBIES

In my spare time my hobbies are ....

....

....

....

....

....

....

....

....

Having hobbies is important to me because ....

....

....

....

....

....

....

....

PLACE
PHOTO HERE

PLACE
PHOTO HERE

PLACE
PHOTO HERE

PLACE
PHOTO HERE

PLACE
PHOTO HERE

PLACE
PHOTO HERE

THE CIRCLE OF LIFE

PLACE
PHOTO HERE

PLACE
PHOTO HERE

GRANDCHILDREN

My first grandchild was born

    On ....

    At ....

The baby was named ....

When I heard the news, I ....

....

....

My other grandchildren are ....

....

....

We play ....

....

....

The thing I love about my grandchildren is ....

....

....

The best thing about being a grandmother is ....

....

....

....

I REMEMBER THE TIME...

PLACE
PHOTO HERE

PLACE
PHOTO HERE

PLACE
PHOTO HERE

MY LIFE NOW...

My favorite things to do now are

My favorite vacation places are

My favorite family memory is

HOW MY LIFE HAS CHANGED

PLACE
PHOTO HERE

PLACE
PHOTO HERE

PLACE
PHOTO HERE

PLACE
PHOTO HERE

This edition published by Cottage Door Press, LLC, in 2020.
First published 2016 by Parragon Books, Ltd.

Copyright © 2020 Cottage Door Press, LLC
5005 Newport Drive, Rolling Meadows, Illinois 60008

Artwork by Jung Suk Hyun used under license from Shutterstock

ISBN: 978-1-68052-906-7

Printed in China

Parragon Books is an imprint of Cottage Door Press, LLC.
Parragon Books® and the Parragon® logo are registered trademarks
of Cottage Door Press, LLC.